IN SEARCH OF RETURNS

Making Sense of Financial Markets

John Looby

Published by Oak Tree Press, Cork T12 EVT0, Ireland

www.oaktreepress.com / www.SuccessStore.com

© 2021 John Looby

A catalogue record of this book is available from the British Library.

ISBN 978 1 78119 511 6 (paperback)
ISBN 978 1 78119 512 3 (ePub)
ISBN 978 1 78119 513 0 (Kindle)
ISBN 978 1 78119 514 7 (PDF)

Cover design: Kieran O'Connor

Cover image: lim_pix / Shutterstock.com

Illustrations: stmartina / fiverr.com; quickcartoon / fiverr.com

Disclaimer: The information contained in this publication does not represent investment advice. Readers should always seek independent professional advice specific to their own requirements before taking any action based on the information provided herein. Neither the author nor the publisher assumes liability for any losses that may be sustained by use of the approaches outlined in this book, and any such liability is hereby disclaimed.

CONTENTS

FIGURES

Acknowledgements

I would like to thank Ian Kehoe of *The Currency* for publishing much of this material originally.

I would also like to thank Joe Looby, Ken Power, Eamonn O'Donoghue, Dan O'Donovan, Joe Mottley and Paul McCarville for commenting on earlier drafts, and of course the always patient Brian O'Kane – long live debate!

Introduction

Theoretically, there are at least two reasons for interest rates to be positive:

- First, the need to compensate lenders for postponing consumption – the time value of money;

- Second, the need to compensate lenders for the varied but unavoidable risk of not being repaid – credit risk.

In practice, from the earliest references to debt in the ancient world, the fact of debtors compensating lenders has been widely accepted. This continued through the classical period and, even in Medieval Europe where usury was forbidden by the Christian Church, interest-bearing loans were the norm.

But in the wake of the Lehman collapse in September 2008, the global economy and banking system faced meltdown. Many feared a re-run of the Great Depression of 1929. This view failed to reckon with the powerful tools available to policymakers.

Crucially, the policy responses to the CoVID-19 pandemic have seen these tools deployed with renewed and expanded aggression.

Negative official interest rates are the new normal in Europe and bond investors at every maturity out to 30 years are all but paying for the privilege of loaning money to many Eurozone governments. More generally, negative real long-term interest rates are now embedded globally.

Figure 1: The ECB Official Interest Rate, 2000 to 2020

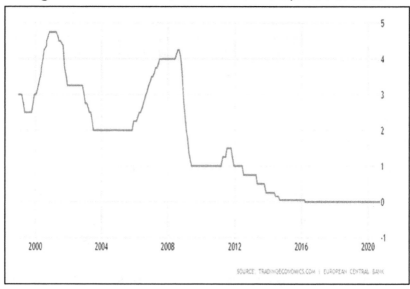

SOURCE: TRADINGECONOMICS.COM | EUROPEAN CENTRAL BANK

Unsurprisingly, the resulting hunt for returns has heightened the lure of financial markets. This recent quote from the *Financial Times* on the striking success of the financial trading platform Robinhood – one among many such services – captures the mood well:

Customers are flocking to the platform – Robinhood has become synonymous with the boom in retail investing that has drawn millions of people to the markets – many for the first time – to join the roaring rally that began in March (2020) and this week pushed the S&P 500 to an all-time high.

As I write today, the gripping dramas of Bitcoin, Tesla, GameStop, chat-boards and day-traders seem everywhere. Anecdotally, there is no doubt that many people here have also joined the fray. With Irish deposit rates going negative and deposit sizes going skyward, it seems timely to consider how such savings might be invested. I hope this guide to making sense of the financial markets will be a helpful contribution.

Note: I will not be covering the seemingly perennial preference of the Irish investor – property.

1

THE ASSET RISK SPECTRUM

Financial markets are helpfully seen as an asset risk spectrum stretching from risk-free assets at one extreme to their riskier counterparts at the other. Correspondingly, the return on offer stretches from the risk-free rate to a rate that reflects the potential gain or loss from bearing risk.

The asset risk spectrum encompasses:

- Bank deposits;
- Government bonds;
- Corporate bonds;
- Stocks;
- Alternative assets;
- Derivatives.

Figure 2: The Asset Risk Spectrum

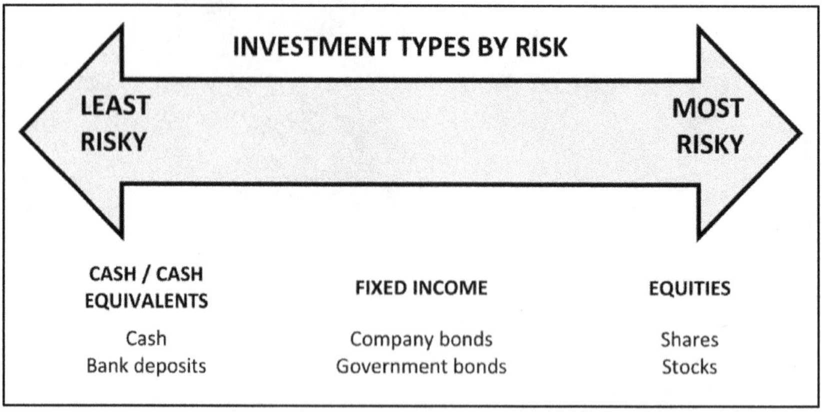

INVESTMENT TYPES BY RISK

LEAST
RISKY

MOST
RISKY

CASH / CASH EQUIVALENTS	FIXED INCOME	EQUITIES
Cash	Company bonds	Shares
Bank deposits	Government bonds	Stocks

Adapted from www.stansberryresearch.com.

Bank Deposits

Traditionally, the risk-free asset in Ireland is a bank deposit generating a risk-free return in the form of deposit interest. Necessarily underwritten by the government and backed in practice by the European Central Bank, the nominal value of bank deposits is effectively guaranteed.

Government Bonds

In like fashion, loaning money to the government *via* an Irish Government bond is also effectively risk-free. Again, given that the investment is underwritten by the government and backed by the European Central Bank, there is little doubt that the interest and capital will be repaid in full and on time.

Corporate Bonds

Moving out the risk spectrum, the next asset is credit or loaning money to companies *via* a corporate bond. While credit markets are a huge part of the financial market landscape across the

Atlantic, they are much less significant in Europe where banks are the main provider of corporate credit.

Importantly, the return here is not risk-free. Loaning money to a company always entails the risk of loss. This is compensated for by the potential, but not the guarantee, of a higher return than the risk-free alternative.

Stocks

Company stocks, shares or equities come next. For the shareholder, they confer a proportionate ownership stake – reflecting the percentage of the shares owned – and a proportionate share of the profits generated.

Crucially, this is profit after the servicing of debt. In the capital structure of the firm, the shareholder ranks behind the creditor / bondholder. Fundamentally, this means that shareholders bear more risk than creditors, and, again, must be compensated by the potential, but not the guarantee, of a higher return.

Alternative Assets

In recent decades, there has been strong growth in so-called alternative assets. This is a heterogenous category that includes everything from private equity to commodities, such as gold or oil. All such alternatives have a correspondingly varied risk and potential return profile and should be positioned on the asset risk spectrum accordingly.

Derivatives

For completeness, it's important to mention derivatives. A derivative is a financial instrument whose value is *derived* from the value of another asset, which is known as the 'underlying'. When the price of the underlying changes, the value of the derivative also changes. Simply put, a derivative is a contract that *derives* its value from changes in the price of the underlying.

Importantly, this contract is often structured to give access to leverage (borrowed money) which will clearly change the risk and potential return exposure.

Summary

The age of risk-free return is over, and the need for a sensible framework to face this challenge arguably has never been greater. Having begun with a brief overview of the asset risk spectrum and where individual assets are positioned on it, the next chapter considers them collectively through the prism of diversification and portfolio theory.

Diversification & Portfolio Theory

The benefit of diversification is often called the only free lunch in investing. The promise of generating the same 'return' while bearing less 'risk' is compelling.

For a simple illustration of this tantalising promise, assume a world where it's either raining or sunny with equal probability, and consider an investor with the following three choices:

- Invest 100% of her capital in a company selling umbrellas

- Invest 100% of her capital in a company selling ice-cream

- Invest 50% of her capital in a company selling umbrellas and 50% of her capital in a company selling ice-cream.

When it's raining, the umbrella company reaps all the profit, while the ice-cream company reaps all the profit when it's sunny. The expected return and the volatility around that expected return for each of the three possible investment choices or 'portfolios' are summarised in **Figure 3**.

Note that the expected return is the weighted average of the expected returns for each asset in the portfolio, while the volatility is a statistical measure (the standard deviation, defined as the dispersion of a dataset around its mean) of the variability around that return – effectively a proxy for risk.

Figure 3: The Effect of Diversification on Returns

	Raining	Sunny	Expected Return	Volatility
Umbrella	100	0	50	25
Ice-cream	0	100	50	25
Umbrellas & Ice-cream	50	50	50	0

The expected return is the same for each of the three possible portfolios but, crucially, the volatility of the return is lower for the choice of investing 50% in the umbrella company and 50% in the ice-cream company. The choice to diversify has generated the same expected return as the other portfolios, while bearing less risk. This seemingly simple insight is at the heart of modern portfolio theory, and its ubiquitous practical workhorse, the Capital Asset Pricing Model.

Modern Portfolio Theory

Developed by a varied group of US academics from the early 1950s, some of whom subsequently received Nobel prizes for their efforts, this widely followed approach has dominated both classrooms and trading rooms for the decades since.

Although often laden with obscure jargon, the basic rationale of the theory can be outlined in four simple steps:

- **Step 1:** To illustrate the risk / return trade-off, modern portfolio theorists created the **Capital Market Line** (**Figure 4**). This is simply the graph of all the portfolios that optimally combine the risk-free rate of return and risky assets. The clear assumption is that the higher the expected return, the higher the risk;

Figure 4: The Capital Market Line

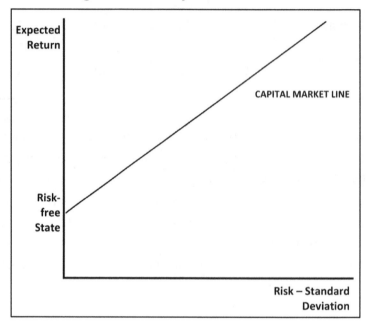

- **Step 2:** The next key assumption is that investors are typically **risk-averse**. In practice, this means that they prefer a certain outcome to an equivalent uncertain gamble. Graphing the relationship between utility (happiness) and wealth in **Figure 5**, the risk-averse investor derives a higher utility from the certainty of $100,000 than the equivalent uncertain alternative of tossing a coin with a 50% chance of winning $50,000 and a 50% chance of winning $150,000 (which gives the same $100,000 expected return);

Figure 5: The Risk-averse Investor

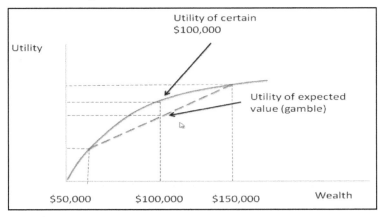

- **Step 3:** Next in the risk / return framework, the assumption of risk aversion is expressed graphically in the **Efficient Frontier** (**Figure 6**) – the curve that maximises expected return for any given level of risk (standard deviation);

Figure 6: The Efficient Frontier

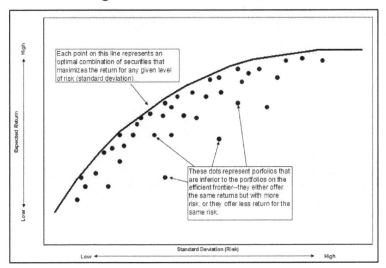

- **Step 4:** Bringing together the free lunch of diversification, the risk / return trade-off of the Capital Market Line, and the assumption of risk aversion underpinning the Efficient Frontier, modern portfolio theory generates an optimal portfolio known as the **Market Portfolio.** Graphically, this is the intercept point of the Capital Market Line and the Efficient Frontier (**Figure 7**);

Figure 7: The Optimal / Market Portfolio

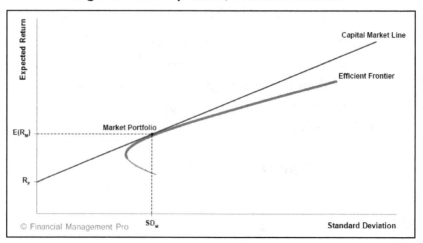

Unfortunately, modern portfolio theory, as expressed in the Capital Asset Pricing Model, is elegant but flawed. The investor Howard Marks summarises the issue with characteristic clarity in his book, *The Most Important Thing – Uncommon Sense for the Thoughtful Investor*:

Especially in good times, far too many people can be overheard saying, "Riskier investments provide higher returns. If you want to make more money, the answer is to take more risk". But riskier investments absolutely cannot be counted on to deliver higher returns. Why not? It's simple: if riskier investments reliably produced higher returns, they wouldn't be riskier.

The correct formulation is that to attract capital, riskier investments have to offer the prospect of higher returns, or higher promised returns, or higher expected returns. But there's absolutely nothing to say those higher prospective returns must materialize.

The way I conceptualize the Capital Market Line makes it easier for me to relate to the relationship underlying it all.

Riskier investments are those for which the outcome is less certain. That is, the probability distribution of returns is wider. When priced fairly, riskier investments should entail: higher expected returns; the possibility of lower returns; and in some cases, the possibility of losses.

*The traditional risk / return trade-off (of Modern Portfolio Theory) is deceptive because it communicates the positive connection between risk and return but fails to suggest the uncertainty involved. I hope my version of the graph (**Figure 8**) is more helpful. It's meant to suggest both the positive relationship between risk and expected return and the fact that uncertainty about the return and the possibility of loss increases as risk increases.*

Figure 8: The Capital Market Line – Risk & Reality

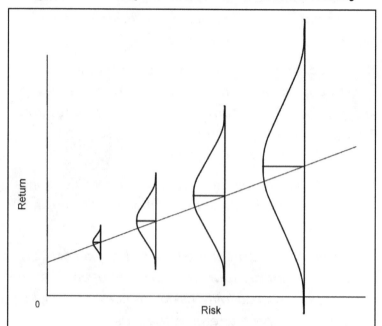

Summary

For investors, the more nuanced outline of risk and reality explained by Howard Marks is not the most significant flaw in modern portfolio theory. The **Efficient Markets Hypothesis**, which we consider in the next chapter, is the winner of that prize.

THE CASE FOR ACTIVE INVESTING

Grounded in modern portfolio theory, the dominant orthodoxy in finance over the past 70 years is the Efficient Markets Hypothesis, whose key conclusion is that trying to beat financial markets is a fool's errand. It argues that, in a process analogous to Brownian motion because market prices jiggle about randomly and instantly discount all new information, it is impossible to beat the market.

In practice, this conclusion has been borne out by many studies over many time periods. As neatly summarised by the academic and investor Bruce Greenwald:

> *Approximately 70% of active professional investors have done worse than they would have by adhering to a passive strategy of simply buying a share of the market*

as a whole – a representative sample of all available securities.

In addition, the fact that the higher cost of paying for active management necessarily tilts the average outcome in favour of the passive alternative clinches the argument for many – see **Figure 9**.

Figure 9: The Zero-sum Game & the Impact of Costs

*Distribution of investor returns **before costs***

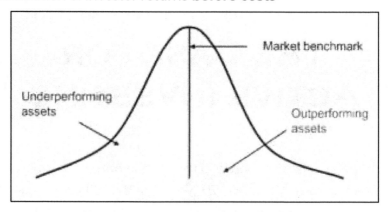

*Distribution of investor returns **after costs***

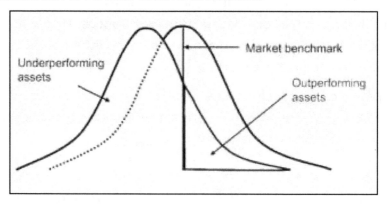

Clearly, beating the market is not easy. In the salty words of Charlie Munger, the long-time business partner of Warren Buffett:

It's not supposed to be easy. Anyone who finds it easy is stupid.

However, despite the uphill challenge, the stunningly successful investment track records of Munger, Buffett and other active investors suggest that the market *can* be beaten – as we'll see in the next chapter. Moreover, they highlight the materially significant reward for those who succeed.

The Power of Compounding

The extraordinary power of compounding is central to that reward. For illustration, **Figure 10** shows that a 3.5% annual return for 50 years produces an increase in wealth by a factor just shy of 6. By comparison, a 7% annual return for 50 years produces an increase in wealth by a factor of almost 30.

Figure 10: The Power of Compounding

Annual Return (%)	1	2	3	4	5	6	7	8	9	10
Doubling Time (years)	70	35	23.3	17.5	14	11.7	10	8.8	7.8	7

Clearly, the greater the excess return, the longer the time-period, the increasingly greater the impact on your long-term wealth. Crucially, many successful active investors have benefitted greatly from the long-term power of compounding,

The attempt to beat the market is not *always* foolhardy. There are inefficiencies in the behaviour of market economies and the financial markets embedded within them. To benefit from the long-term power of compounding, the active investor has a strong incentive to exploit them.

The Financial Instability Hypotheses

The period from the end of the Cold War until the onset of the Global Financial Crisis in 2008 seemed to validate the modern macroeconomic framework, and its close cousin, the Efficient Markets Hypothesis. The march of globalisation, technology, financial innovation, and free-market ideology seemed to have produced a great moderation in the behaviour of the global economy.

For global financial markets and policymakers, the tantalising prospect in the words of then UK Chancellor, Gordon Brown, that "we have eliminated boom and bust" finally seemed more than a theoretical aspiration. The conviction that financial markets are the rational and efficient discounters of all public information grew in parallel.

The following quote from Nobel Laureate in Economics Robert Lucas, in his Presidential Address to the American Economic Association in 2003, gives a good flavour for the extent to which this framework and its implications had gained wide acceptance:

> *My thesis in this lecture is that macroeconomics in its original sense has succeeded: Its central problem of*

depression prevention has been solved, for all practical purposes, and has in fact been solved for many decades.

When this optimism proved delusional and the most serious financial and economic crisis since the Great Depression erupted, the need for a more realistic framework was laid bare.

The Financial Instability Hypothesis of long-neglected US economist, Hyman Minsky, first published in 1975, gained a fresh following as a more plausible description of how a dynamic market economy behaves in practice.

In particular, the characterisation by Minsky of the macro economy as a system prone to bouts of dramatic instability generated endogenously by the financial system chimed well in the dramatic days up to and after the collapse of Lehman Brothers. The key insight that stability can lead to instability plausibly captured the long post-Cold War experience and its shuddering *dénouement*.

By contrast, the equilibrium-seeking system of modern macroeconomics, where such instability is impossible, was exposed as a flawed framework dangerously divorced from reality. In like fashion, the fallibility of the Efficient Markets Hypothesis also was exposed.

The shock of this realisation was famously expressed by legendary Federal Reserve Chairman, Alan Greenspan, who told a congressional committee in October 2008:

Yes, I've found a flaw (in my ideology). I don't know how significant or permanent it is. But I've been very distressed by that fact. The modern risk management paradigm held sway for decades. The whole intellectual edifice, however, collapsed in the summer of last year.

The Rise of the Behaviouralists

The Nobel committee deciding on the 2002 award of the Memorial Prize in Economics chose to break with tradition by awarding the prize to a psychologist: Daniel Kahneman.

Primarily for his seminal paper with Amos Tversky in 1974, *Judgement under Uncertainty: Heuristics and Biases*, the award was an acknowledgement of how their work had powerfully shaken the key assumptions underpinning modern macroeconomics and finance. Most particularly, the compelling portrayal of human decision-making as being littered with systematic short-cuts and biases casts great doubt over the key assumption of probability-weighted 'rationality'.

More recently, a broad and growing range of research has further strengthened the argument that the market is not wholly efficient and therefore can be beaten. For example, in a speech to the London School of Economics, *Herd Behaviour and Keeping up with the Joneses*, ploughing a different, if related, furrow to Kahneman, Andrew Oswald outlined the key insight of how *individual rationality* can often be consistent with *collective catastrophe*.

Taking his lead from the animal kingdom, Oswald argued that because human happiness is a function of relative rather than absolute position within a group, herding or clustering behaviour is the rational response of individuals to most situations. With a range of examples from fashion to frogs, he makes a powerful case that humans are frightened of falling behind and are consequently prompted to constantly adjust their relative position within a group, just as an animal seeking safety will do likewise in a herd.

As with the herd however, this individually rational behaviour on occasion can lead to collective catastrophe. The stark image from Thomas Hardy of the flock of sheep plunging to their collective deaths, rationally following each other over the cliff to maintain their relative position, has clear implications for investors.

Summary

The trend toward passive investment is strong and not surprising. For those who believe that the market can't be beaten, or even if it can that it's prohibitively difficult to try, investing in passive strategies makes sense. By doing so however, they are eschewing the possibility of a significantly better outcome.

The evidence and rationale that the market can be beaten is compelling. If successful, the power of compounding makes the active approach significantly more rewarding. The search for a credible approach that gives a good probability of success is therefore worthwhile. The next chapter considers the case for value investing.

THE CASE FOR VALUE INVESTING

The widely acknowledged father of value investing was an American academic, investor and author, Ben Graham, and the widely acknowledged founding text of the discipline is the book he published with David Dodd in 1934, *Security Analysis*.

Famously, Warren Buffett was a student of Graham at Columbia University in the 1940s and has turned his value investing prowess into one of the greatest fortunes ever.

In addition to being a legendary investor, Buffett is also a prolific writer. Arguably, one of his most significant pieces was published in the Columbia Business School magazine in the autumn of 1984: *The Super-investors of Graham & Doddsville*.

In this piece, Buffett makes a compelling case that the incredible, long-term success of a disparate group of investors (see **Figure 11**) could not be a function of random luck and had to be due to their commonly-shared value investing philosophy.

Figure 11: The Super-investors' Returns

Fund	Manager	Fund Period	Fund Return *p.a.*
Pacific Partners Limited	Rick Guerin	1965 to 1983	**32.9%**
Buffett Partnership	Warren Buffett	1957 to 1969	**29.5%**
Perlmeter investments	Stan Perlmeter	1965 to 1983	**23.0%**
Washington Post Fund	3 different managers	1978 to 1983	**21.8%**
WJS Limited	Walter J Schloss	1956 to 1984	**21.3%**
TEK Limited	Tom Knapp	1968 to 1983	**20.0%**
Charles Munger Limited	Charles Munger	1962 to 1975	**19.8%**
Sequoia Fund	William J Ruane	1970 to 1984	**18.2%**
FMC Pension Fund	8 different managers	1975 to 1983	**17.1%**

The previous chapter emphasised the power of compounding. Crucially, many successful value investors have benefitted greatly from the long-term power of compounding,

Value does not equal Price

The fundamental tenet of value investing is that value does not equal price. Consequent on that, the market *can* be beaten.

Value investing fundamentally rejects Modern Finance Theory, and the key assumptions underpinning the Efficient Markets Hypothesis. By contrast, it rightfully can claim to be a forerunner of the breakthroughs in behavioural economics and finance pioneered in recent decades by the likes of Daniel Kahneman, Richard Thaler, Robert Schiller, and others.

As stock investors, we should always remember that we are owners of a share in a business and that the value of the business to us is ultimately determined by the cash that we take out of it.

In practice, the challenge is to make a credible assessment of what Buffett calls 'intrinsic value':

> *Intrinsic value can be defined simply: it is the discounted value of the cash that can be taken out of a business during its remaining life. As our definition suggests, intrinsic value is an estimate rather than a precise figure and two people looking at the same set of facts will almost inevitably come up with different intrinsic value figures.*

Before investing, the challenge is to apply Graham & Dodd's approach – built on since by their followers, such as Buffett – to estimating intrinsic value. Only then can a decision be made as to whether this value is sufficiently attractive relative to its market price to warrant an investment.

Importantly, the choice of a discount rate (which reflects the time value of money) is an unavoidable decision in the valuing of any asset, linking the value to the cash the asset will generate in the future. Everything else being equal, the lower the discount rate, the higher the value and *vice versa*.

A key ingredient in the calculation of an 'appropriate' discount rate is the rate on offer from a broadly 'risk-free' alternative such as a 10-year government bond. Again, everything else being equal, the lower the yield, the higher the asset value and *vice versa*.

In his letter to Berkshire Hathaway shareholders in 1998, Buffett summarised his approach to this key decision:

> *We don't discount the future cash flows (of our stock holdings) at 9% or 10%; we use the US treasury rate. We try to deal with things about which we are quite certain. You can't compensate for risk by using a high discount rate.*

While different value investors often arrive at different decisions by using different techniques or differ on the importance accorded to the various inputs to their valuations, they are united in their goal to seek and exploit the difference between value and price.

Importantly, value investing is constantly evolving and should not be viewed as a narrow focus on specific metrics. For example, just having a low Price to Book or low Price to Earnings ratio should not necessarily be defined as the same as buying something for less than its intrinsic value. Much recent commentary on the alleged poor performance of 'value investing' really means the poor performance of low Price to Book investing.

Mr Market

A particularly useful tool for thinking about the divergence between value and price is the Graham creation of *Mr Market*.

In varying moods swinging from greed to fear, *Mr Market* shows up every day offering to buy and sell you securities at constantly changing prices. As a value investor, this is your opportunity. Your goal is to exploit the moods of *Mr Market* to buy and sell at prices different from your assessment of value and to do so with as large a margin of safety as possible.

But narrowly seeking value alone can be misleading. Many poor businesses are 'cheap' for good reasons, and many great businesses are sometimes available at 'good' prices. To help avoid the former while finding the latter, the successful value investor also seeks quality.

In seeking quality, the words of Buffett quoted by Laurence Cunningham in his book, *Essays of Warren Buffett*, are especially helpful:

> *In each case we try to buy into businesses with*
> *favourable long-term economics. Our goal is to find an*
> *outstanding business at a sensible price. Charlie and I*
> *have found that making silk purses out of silk is the best*
> *we can do; with sows' ears we fail.*
>
> *It must be noted your chairman, always a quick study,*
> *required only 20 years to recognise how important it is to*
> *buy good businesses. In the interim, I searched for*

*'bargains' and had misfortune to find some. My
punishment was an education in the economics of short
line farm implement manufacturers, third place
department stores and New England textile
manufacturers.*

*In addition, we think the very term 'value investing' is
redundant. What is investing if it is not the act of seeking
value at least sufficient to justify the amount paid?
Growth benefits investors only when the businesses in
point can invest at incremental returns that are enticing.
In other words, only when each dollar used to finance
growth creates over a dollar of long-term market value.*

The Buffett case for quality is illustrated by a simple quantitative
example of how quality is fundamentally determined by returns.

Assume an investment of $100 million, where the cost of funds
(and thus the required return) is 10%. **Figure 12** shows the
impact of various levels of return.

Figure 12: The Impact of Quality on Returns

	Case A	Case B	Case C
Return on investment	5%	10%	20%
Return on investment	$5m	$10m	$10m
Cost of investment	$10m	$10m	$10m
Net income created	($5m)	0	$10m
Impact	Value destroyed	No value	Value created

Summary

For stock investors, the lessons are clear:

- Investing at a competitive disadvantage destroys value;

- Investing on a level playing field neither creates nor destroys value;

- Only investing with a return greater than the cost of funds / required return creates value.

In the timeless words of Buffett:

Time is the friend of a wonderful business, the enemy of the mediocre.

The case for value investing with an appreciation of quality is convincing. Value does not equal price, the market can be beaten, and the way to beat it is to exploit the moods of *Mr Market*. If successful, the power of compounding then will ensure a profoundly positive effect on your long-term wealth. Many value investors have succeeded, and with the right mindset, we have a chance to join them.

Helpfully, the thoughts of a towering contemporary thinker chime with the mindset needed to exploit the changing moods of *Mr Market*. The next chapter explores the thoughts of Nassim Nicholas Taleb and the mindset of value investing.

Nassim Nicholas Taleb & The Value Investing Mindset

The philosopher, options-trader, and best-selling author, Nassim Nicholas Taleb, is among the most provocative and original thinkers of our time.

Across many domains, his insights on how we are persistently prone to being 'fooled by randomness', blind-sided by 'the black swan', and tethered to the 'fragile' are central to understanding the world in which we live. They also chime loudly with the mindset of a value investor.

Luck *v* Skill / Noise *v* Signal & Time

I'm sure there are many golfers, tennis-players and football fans reading this today:

- For the golfers, consider whether your chance of beating Rory McIlroy is greater after playing a hole, a round, or a tournament?

- For the tennis players, whether your chance of beating Rafael Nadal is greater after playing a point, a game, or a set?

- For the football fans, whether the chance of Chelsea lying ahead of West Brom in the Premier League table is greater at Hallowe'en, at Christmas, or at the end of the season?

The signal is that McIlroy is a more skilful golfer than you, Nadal a more skilful tennis player and Chelsea – though it pains me to say so – a more skilful team than West Brom. Crucially, the longer the time frame considered, the greater the likelihood of skill trumping luck – of signal trumping noise.

Taleb cites the typically provocative example of Russian roulette, where clearly any tendency to confuse luck with skill inevitably will end with a fatal outcome.

What is true of golf, tennis, football, and Russian roulette is also true of investing. For many, it is the most crucial part of the value investing mindset, as succinctly stated by the great Canadian investor, Peter Cundhill:

> *The most important attribute for success in value investing is patience, patience, and more patience; most investors do not possess this characteristic.*

The Futility of Prediction

Taleb is probably best known for his conviction that prediction is futile, captured in his memorable parable of the turkey in the run-up to Christmas Day.

Every day is a great day for the turkey – he's got lots to eat, lots to drink, he's very well looked after. As each day goes by, the turkey becomes more and more convinced that this is the way life should be – he should have lots to eat, he should have lots to drink and he should be very well looked after. But, sometime late in Christmas week – bang! The turkey is dead and heading for the oven. **Figure 13** translates this into an investment graph.

Figure 13: The Anatomy of a Blow-up

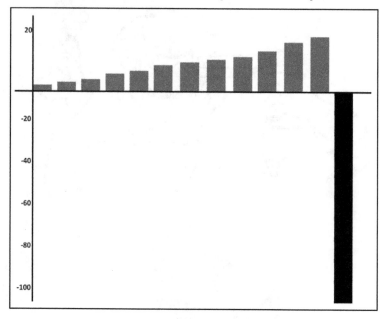

Tellingly, Warren Buffett also famously ignores prediction, avoids the 'turkey' problem, and warns:

> *Forecasts may tell you a great deal about the forecaster;*
> *they tell you nothing about the future.*

The Benefit of a Buffer

Taleb also makes a compelling case for the benefit of a buffer – a margin of safety. He argues that any system, entity, or approach that has a buffer / margin of safety has an often critically greater chance of survival and success. The example he gives is that of evolution, conferring two kidneys on the human body, as a buffer against the otherwise fatal consequences of losing one.

The widely lauded value investor, Seth Klarman of Baupost, is such a believer in the importance of a buffer when investing, that he named his major book on the subject, *Margin of Safety: Risk-averse Investing Strategies for the Thoughtful Investor*, arguing that:

> ... *a margin of safety is necessary because valuation is an imprecise art, the future is unpredictable, and investors are human and do make mistakes.*

Anti-Fragile – Benefiting from Unpredictability

The next of Taleb's concepts that resonates powerfully with the mindset of a value investor is the more subtle one of anti-fragility – benefitting from unpredictability.

Anti-fragility is probably best understood by first considering its opposite – the fragile. Taleb uses the example of a china cup sitting on a wooden table at a substantial height above a stone floor. While we have no idea when or why – or, indeed, whether – the cup will fall from the table, we do know that when it does it will smash across the unforgiving floor. The cup is fragile – it doesn't like unpredictability, disorder, or crucially, time.

Taleb defines the anti-fragile as simply the opposite – that which likes unpredictability, disorder, and time. This concept of anti-fragility captures what is arguably the most important Taleb insight of all:

> *Knowing that you cannot predict does not mean that*
> *you cannot benefit from unpredictability.*

It is no coincidence that Buffett has been a consistent beneficiary of unpredictability – a consistent beneficiary of anti-fragility:

- After centuries of profitability, the Lloyds' insurance 'names' go bust – Buffett benefits;

- Hurricane Katrina devastates New Orleans – Buffett benefits;

- The Global Financial Crisis rocks Goldman Sachs and Swiss Re – Buffett benefits

- The VHI finally runs out of regulatory road – Buffett benefits.

Buffett had no idea that Piper Alpha would explode, that Katrina would devastate New Orleans, that the Global Financial Crisis would erupt, or that the VHI would suddenly need capital, but he was positioned to benefit from each of these unpredictable events. In Taleb terms, he was anti-fragile.

Taleb & Pabrai

Finally, it's important to highlight the echo of Taleb in the approach of the stunningly successful value investor, Mohnish Pabrai.

Pabrai began his career as a technology professional, but switched to investing after discovering Warren Buffett in 1994. Since then he has generated an annualised investment return of over 20% and has been the managing partner of the Pabrai Investment Funds since their launch in 1999.

In his disarmingly readable book, *The Dhando Investor*, Pabrai grounds his investment approach and success in the story of the forced migration of the ethnic Indian population from Uganda to the United States in 1972. Effectively ordered penniless out of Uganda at gunpoint by the dictator Idi Amin, many of the fleeing migrants achieved remarkable economic success in their new home by following a clearly defined approach to business and investing.

The Dhando approach is a Guajarati concept that roughly translates into seeking exposure to great potential upside with little downside, or as Pabrai memorably puts it in his book, seeking exposures characterised by a 'Heads I win, Tails I don't lose much' payoff.

The echo of Taleb is clear and powerful. In his 2012 essay, *Understanding is a Poor Substitute for Convexity (Anti-fragility)*, Taleb provides the telling insight and image:

> *... in complex systems, ones in which we have little visibility of the chains of cause-consequences, tinkering, bricolage, or similar variations of trial and error have been shown to vastly outperform – it is nature's modus operandi. But tinkering needs to be convex; it is imperative. Take the most opaque of all, cooking, which relies entirely on the heuristics of trial and error, as it has not been possible for us to design a dish directly from chemical equations or reverse-engineer a taste from nutritional labels. We take hummus, add an ingredient, say a spice, taste to see if there is an improvement from the complex interaction, and retain if we like the addition or discard the rest. **Critically we have the option, not the obligation, to keep the result, which allows us to retain the upper bound and be unaffected by adverse outcomes.***

Figure 14 illustrates what Taleb means by 'convex'. The performance curves outward; anywhere such asymmetry prevails, we can call it convex; otherwise we are in a concave position. The implication is that, in a convex position, you are harmed much less by an error (or a variation) than you can benefit from it.

In quoting an old Yiddish proverb, Taleb captures the essence of what helpfully can be thought of as the Dhando approach to antifragility:

> *Provide for the worst; the best can take care of itself.*

Figure 14: More Gain than Pain

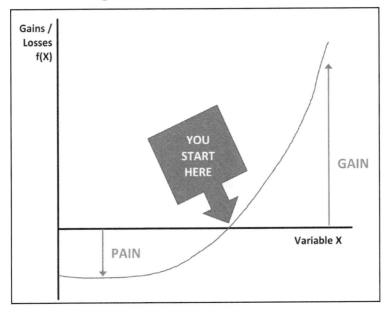

Source: https://www.edge.org/conversation/nassim_nicholas_taleb-
understanding-is-a-poor-substitute-for-convexity-antifragility.

Summary

To exploit the changing moods of *Mr Market*, Taleb's thoughts help illuminate and guide. Resonating strongly with the great value investors, they increase our likelihood of developing the right mindset for success. The focus of the next chapter is the significant cost of a particularly flawed mindset: The Dumb Money Effect.

6

THE DUMB MONEY
EFFECT

Financial markets are increasingly dominated by faster and cheaper information, faster and cheaper trading, and ever-shorter time-horizons. Every morsel of news is instantly blasted across multiple platforms, sparking a frenzied trading response.

Unfortunately, the frenzied activity, and the stories that drive it, are a very costly distraction for investors. When markets are down, they become fearful and withdraw their cash. To compound the problem, when markets are up, they become greedy and add more cash. This pattern of investor behaviour is so consistent that academics have a name for it: The Dumb Money Effect.

The Boston-based consulting firm Dalbar tracks the wide margin between investment returns – the return of a benchmark index – and the significantly smaller returns captured by the average investor. For example, the S&P 500 returned an average of 10% per year for the 30 years ending December 2019, while the average annual return of stock fund investors in the US was just 6%. Strikingly, the average investor lags the market by a significant margin over all time periods.

This result was echoed in a similar study in 2014 by the investment bank, Credit Suisse.

> *For the 20 years up to the end of 2013, the investor return in actively managed funds was just 60% to 80% of the return recorded by actively managed funds ... investors who own actively managed funds earn lower returns than the funds themselves.*

Clearly, investors should ignore the allure of short-term stories and resist the temptation to jump in and out of the market. Their persistent compunction to trade too often costs them dearly. Notwithstanding the evidence, the instinct to chase noise – and thus to damage wealth – continues to dominate.

Behavioural Economics

As noted earlier, the Nobel committee deciding on the 2002 award of the Memorial Prize in Economics chose to break with tradition by awarding the prize to a psychologist: Daniel Kahneman. Although a controversial choice among economists, it was a significant acknowledgement of the growing importance of the field of behavioural economics pioneered by Kahneman, and his late colleague, Amos Tversky.

Behavioural economics is a relatively new field that grapples with the seemingly systemic irrationality of decision-makers in many domains. While the likes of Keynes, Minsky and others were certainly interested in such behaviour, its recent flourishing can be traced to the 1974 paper by Kahneman and Tversky, *Judgement under Uncertainty: Heuristics and Biases.*

Fifteen years later, the Nobel committee conferred further recognition on behavioural economics by choosing Richard Thaler as the recipient of the Memorial Prize in 2017. Inspired by Kahneman, Thaler is credited with bringing behavioural economics into the mainstream. His 2008 bestselling book with Cass Sunstein, *Nudge*, and their subsequent input into public policy in the US and the UK, have successfully promoted behavioural economics to a wide and growing audience.

More recently, his book *Misbehaving: The Making of Behavioural Economics* is a wonderfully readable account of his thinking from its initial Kahneman-inspired roots in the 1970s up to the present day.

In a paper with Shlomo Benartzi in 1995, Thaler identified the crucial behavioural trait of 'myopic loss aversion'. First, Thaler & Benartzi noted the findings of Kahneman and others that investors are 'loss-averse' – they are more sensitive to losses than to gains:

> *... empirical estimates of loss aversion are typically in the neighbourhood of 2, meaning that the disutility of giving something up is twice as great as the utility of acquiring it.*

Second, they noted that even investors with a long-term horizon tend to evaluate their portfolios frequently. They call the combination of these two traits 'myopic loss aversion'.

Among much else, 'myopic loss aversion' convincingly explains the persistent performance lag highlighted by Dalbar and

Credit Suisse. Significantly more sensitive to losses than gains, and increasingly driven by an accelerating news-cycle to evaluate their portfolios, investors are persistently destroying their wealth.

Under some plausible assumptions about the allocation between stocks and bonds in a typical portfolio, Thaler & Benartzi conclude that, to avoid the wealth-destroying impact of myopic loss aversion, investors should limit their portfolio evaluation to no more than once a year. Unfortunately, few are likely to heed his advice.

Summary

Among many interesting observations in a fascinating interview titled *Big Data, Intuition and Decision-making in Finance*, Kahneman offered the sobering insight that, in making decisions, most people persistently behave as if 'evidence is not all that compelling'.

Unsurprisingly, the legendary investor Warren Buffett is one of the exceptions. With a typically memorable image in his 2013 letter to fellow shareholders in Berkshire Hathaway, Buffett broadly repeated Thaler & Benartzi's advice:

> *Games are won by players who focus on the playing field, not by those whose eyes are glued to the scoreboard.*

The next chapter focuses on an area of the stock market where many investors have felt very dumb many times: banks.

BANKS ARE DIFFERENT

Bank shareholders have had a tough time. Squeezed margins and weighty regulation have dampened profit and potential for traditional banks around the globe. In contrast to buoyant stock markets more generally, the absolute and relative decline in their share prices has followed inexorably.

Some argue that bank shares are now 'cheap' and represent an attractive investment opportunity, in many cases trading below the balance sheet valuation of their equity. Therefore these commentators argue that even a modest improvement in business performance would spark a sharp rebound in bank share prices. They may well be right. But before committing hard-earned savings in the hope of such returns, a deeper ponder is advisable.

Banks are different. They are structurally vulnerable to crisis. Taking on board Taleb's lesson about fragility, we can't know when or where the next banking crisis will occur, but we do know that, with their current structure, there will be one.

The then Governor of the Bank of England, Sir Mervyn King, summarised this memorably at a speech in New York in 2010, *Banking – from Bagehot to Basel and Back Again*:

> *Banking crises are endemic to the market economy that has evolved since the Industrial Revolution. The words 'banking' and 'crisis' are natural bedfellows. If love and marriage go together like a horse and carriage, then banking and crisis go together like Oxford and the Isis, intertwined for as long as anyone can remember.*

The fundamental difference between banks and other businesses is their capital structure. In comparison to almost any other business, banks are overwhelmingly funded by debt. This has not always been the case, but it has become their defining feature over the past few decades.

For example, in less than four decades in the run-up to the Global Financial Crisis, bank assets in the UK as a % of GDP – overwhelmingly funded by debt to depositors, bondholders and each other – exploded by a factor greater than five.

Figure 15: UK Banking Assets as % of GDP

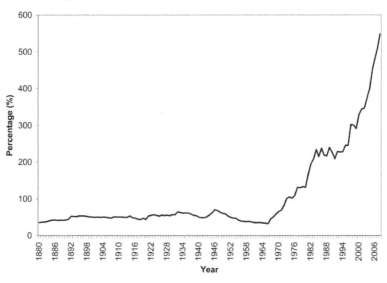

Source: Andrew G Haldane, Bank of England, 2009.

The following comments by Sir Mervyn King from the same speech in 2010 capture this reality well:

The size of the balance sheet (of banks) is no longer limited by the scale of opportunities to lend to companies or individuals in the real economy. So-called 'financial engineering' allows banks to manufacture additional assets without limit.

While banks' balance sheets have exploded, so have the risks associated with those balance sheets. Capital ratios have declined, and leverage has risen. Immediately prior to the crisis, leverage in the banking system of the industrialised world had increased to astronomical levels. Simple leverage ratios of close to 50 or more could be found in the US, UK, and the continent of Europe.

The size, concentration and riskiness of banks have increased in an extraordinary fashion and would be unrecognisable to Bagehot.

Endogenous Money / Asset / Liability Creation

In 1975, in *Money: Whence It Came, Where It Went*, JK Galbraith wrote:

The process by which banks create money is so simple that it repels the mind.

To Galbraith's wry amusement, the money or asset / liability creation process is scarily simple:

- Borrower looks for loan;

- Bank grants loan;

- Loan creates deposit;

- Borrower spends deposit;

- Bank pockets the difference between interest received on its loans (assets) and interest paid on its deposits (liabilities);

- Bank has a compelling incentive to repeat this process as often and in as big a size as possible;

- Bank faces no effective constraint in its compunction to exploit this compelling incentive;

- Central bank is a largely passive accommodator of this money creation power of the private banking system.

As a direct consequence, it is hardly surprising that bank assets and liabilities – their balance sheets – have exploded since Nixon finally broke Bretton Woods and effectively cut money free in 1971 (see **Chapter 8**).

The fundamental point is that private banks create most of our money (and their assets / liabilities) out of thin air. The small amount of paper printed or coin minted is all but irrelevant.

Despite the widespread commitment to reform in the wake of the financial crisis and the extensive measures put in place since, private banking and its money / asset / liability creation capacity remains fundamentally unchanged:

- Banks still have a compelling incentive to expand their balance sheets;

- Bank assets are still supported by a relatively small sliver of equity;

- Banks still run the risk of a dangerous mis-match between their assets and their debts;

- Banks still rely on the backing of central banks and ultimately governments.

There is little reason to believe that the long association between the words 'banking' and 'crisis' is materially looser today than before the crisis.

As summarised recently in the *Financial Times* by Martin Wolf:

> *Today, banks are less leveraged and better supervised than before the crisis. In the UK retail banking is also ringfenced. Yet, the banks are leveraged at about 20 to 1: if the value of their assets falls by 5% or more, such a bank becomes insolvent.*

Summary

The key message for investors is that the risk borne by equity investors in a bank is of a fundamentally different order than that borne in almost any other business.

That is not to say that there won't be times when buying bank shares will prove profitable. Nor is it to say that now isn't one of those times. The message is simply that banks are different and, as investors, we need to treat them differently.

The next chapter will consider the foreign exchange market, and the perennial challenge of managing exchange rate exposure.

MANAGING FOREIGN EXCHANGE RATES & EXPOSURE

For investors, a choice to limit exposure to domestic currency is not tenable. The range of assets excluded is just too wide. Consequently, they must consider the foreign exchange market, and the perennial challenge of managing exchange rate exposure.

Today, most currencies float freely or are managed by their country's Central Bank to maintain a close relationship with the US dollar. The most important example of this is China, where – notwithstanding the political noise of recent years – the People's Bank of China keeps the RMB closely aligned to the dollar.

Importantly, this broadly floating exchange rate era is relatively recent. Before grappling with the investment challenge of how to manage it, we need to understand how we got here.

Gold & Bretton Woods

The gold standard was the effective global monetary regime from well before its formal adoption by Great Britain in 1717 to the shutting of the gold window by US President Richard Nixon in 1971. While its operation was sometimes suspended, or tweaked, in response to war, revolution or depression, the general adherence of most of the globe to this fixed intrinsic standard was a largely unquestioned constant in political, economic, and social life.

The reason for this was the widespread conviction summarised memorably by JM Keynes in his 1919 book, *The Economic Consequences of the Peace*:

> *Lenin was right. There is no subtler, no surer means of overturning the existing basis of society than to debauch the currency. The process engages all the hidden forces of economic law on the side of destruction and does it in a manner which not one man in a million can diagnose.*

To avoid such a sinister calamity, few questioned the basic rationale of the gold standard, and the seemingly obvious observation of the legendary financier JP Morgan in 1893:

> *Gold is money. Everything else is credit.*

In more recent times, the monetary structure of the post-war world constructed at the famous Bretton Woods conference in

July 1944 clearly adhered to this age-old standard. The 44 countries at Bretton Woods agreed to peg their currencies to the US dollar, which in turn was pegged to gold at a rate of $35 per ounce. In effect, the monetary structure of the world was now anchored to the dollar, which in turn was anchored to gold.

The critical outcome of Bretton Woods was that the world needed dollars. In practical terms, this meant that, until the world could sell its goods and services to US buyers to receive dollars or regain its creditworthiness with US banks to borrow them, the enlightened self-interest of US policy was content to all but give them away.

Marshall Aid, broad support for the nascent European Coal and Steel Community, and the preferential trade access afforded to Japan and others, were just some of the policies designed to supply much needed dollars to a desperate world.

Against this backdrop of monetary stability and enlightened US self-interest, post-war global trade expanded rapidly – helping to fuel a remarkable and sustained global recovery. Fondly remembered by many, the post-war decades up to the early 1970s were a golden era of social and economic progress across much of the free world.

The chink in this structure proved to be the implicit necessity for the anchor country, the United States, to manage its economy so that its peg to gold remained credible. Those who held dollars needed to believe that their dollars would always be convertible into gold: the anchor store of value.

Dragged ever deeper into the costly folly of the Vietnam War, and facing a growing balance of payments deficit as well as a quickening flow of dollars to the rest of the world, Nixon fatally undermined the credibility of the dollar link to gold. While the impossible dreams of his predecessor – to build a 'Great Society' at home, while fighting an increasingly expensive and futile war in South East Asia – certainly contributed, the fateful decision was ultimately made by Nixon.

By the early autumn 1971, the persistent appearance of France and other creditors at the gold window in Washington, seeking to convert their growing stock of dollars into gold, left him facing an unenviable choice on that hot August night a mere generation ago. He could continue to convert the dollars presented into gold and thereby exhaust the gold reserves of the United States, or refuse to do so, and smash the cornerstone of the global monetary structure.

Nixon chose the latter and so, having effectively been a constant in human affairs for over a quarter of a millennium, the gold standard formalised by Newton in London in 1717 and subsequently adopted around the globe, was ended by Presidential *fiat* in Washington.

For investors, our era of broadly floating exchange rates, and the necessity of managing exchange rate exposure had dawned.

Managing Exchange Rate Exposure

For many investors, the challenge of managing exchange rate exposure begins with trying to forecast them. While there are lots of approaches, most attempts to forecast foreign exchange rates involves one of the following:

- **Purchasing power parity** (PPP) is perhaps the most widely known approach due to its prominence in most economic textbooks. The PPP forecasting approach is based on the theoretical *Law of One Price*, which states that identical goods in different countries should have identical prices. Based on this underlying principle, the PPP approach forecasts that the exchange rate will change to offset price changes due to inflation. For example, suppose that prices in the UK are expected to increase by 4% over the next year, while prices in the Eurozone are expected to rise by only 2%. The inflation differential between the two is: 4% – 2% = 2%. This means that prices in the UK are expected to rise faster relative to prices in the Eurozone. In this situation, the purchasing power parity approach would forecast that Sterling would have to depreciate by 2% to keep prices between both currency areas relatively equal;

- The **relative economic strength** approach looks at the strength of economic growth in different countries to forecast the direction of exchange rates. The rationale behind this approach is based on the idea that a strong economic environment and potentially high growth is more likely to attract investments from foreign investors. To purchase investments in the desired country, an investor would have to purchase the country's currency – creating increased demand that should cause the currency to appreciate. Unlike the PPP approach, the relative economic strength approach doesn't forecast a precise exchange rate. Rather, this approach gives a general sense of whether a currency is going to appreciate or depreciate and an overall feel for the strength of the expected movement;

- The final approach worth highlighting is the **time series model / charting**. This approach is purely technical in nature and is not based on any economic theory. The rationale is that past behaviour and price patterns can be analysed to predict future price behaviour and patterns. The data used is simply a time series of the exchange rate being analysed to create a model / chart of 'price' through time.

Summary

Unfortunately – as with all forecasting – none of these approaches or, indeed, any of the alternatives are sustainably reliable. There are just too many interacting and unpredictable factors at play.

For this reason, many companies and investors simply hedge their exchange rate exposure. While this seems to offer a simple solution to the challenge, stock investors need to consider two further complications:

- The likelihood that the companies in which they invest are earning non-domestic currency and therefore also might be managing their exchange rate exposure.

- Stock prices respond to exchange rate changes. In recent years, for example, for investors owning UK listed stocks with significant non-UK earnings, the relative decline of Sterling has generally been offset by the appreciation of the stock prices.

In truth, the decision to hedge or not is complicated. For most long-term investors, the best decision arguably is to accept their inability to forecast, while also accepting that hedging is a poor solution.

Like much else in investing, exchange rate exposure is an unavoidable, if uncomfortable, part of the landscape. The next chapter touches on a few of the other challenges looming large as we face the ever uncertain future.

LOOMING CHALLENGES

Investing was a rollercoaster in 2020. Arguably more than ever, the wrenching reality of radical uncertainty dominated all. While the future looms as unknowable as ever, this chapter touches on some of the challenges likely to continue to loom large.

Stock Investing: Beyond the Tangible

The growing importance of the intangible economy is explored in a fascinating recent book by Jonathan Haskel and Stian Westlake: *Capitalism without Capital: The Rise of the Intangible Economy.*

In a thorough treatment of a crucial issue, they outline what they call the quiet revolution of the past two decades, which has seen the major developed economies move to invest more in intangible assets like design, branding, R&D and software, than in tangible assets like machinery, buildings and computers. Furthermore, Haskel & Stian contend that, for all sorts of businesses, from tech firms and pharma companies to coffee shops and gyms, the ability to deploy assets that we can neither see nor touch is increasingly the main source of long-term success.

Unsurprisingly, this change presents profound challenges for investors. When the father of value investing, Ben Graham, formalised his approach with David Dodd in the now iconic book *Security Analysis* in 1934, he made clear his goal of buying stocks at a discount to their net current assets (in other words, cash and other assets that can be turned into cash within one year, such as accounts receivable and inventory, less all liabilities).

In advocating this famous 'Net / Net' approach to stock investing, Graham was attaching little or no value to any long-term tangible assets that a firm might possess. For many who studied and ultimately followed Graham, the extreme conservatism of such an approach became increasingly questionable as they grew comfortable in their ability to assign a value to long-term tangible assets such as Property, Plant and Equipment.

As the memory of the Great Depression faded, the stock market began to re-rate upwards in the 1950s and 1960s, leaving fewer Net / Net stocks. Investors such as the legendary Walter Schloss broadened the search for cheap stocks to buying stocks at a discount to their net tangible assets. Although a less conservative approach than Net / Net, this liquidation valuation approach, where only tangible assets are assigned a value, subsequently has been viewed as overly restrictive.

Today, it is no exaggeration to say that stock investing is increasingly about the assessment of the intangible. For example, with operating assets of around $30bn each, the market value of Apple and Alphabet is now over $2tn and over $1tn, respectively.

Interestingly, some well-known disciples of Graham such as Mohnish Pabrai, Amarath Damoradan, John Huber and Pat Dorsey are notable shareholders in both companies, and famously, Warren Buffett has a substantial shareholding in Apple. Although inspired by the value investing *credo* of Graham, these investors clearly have adapted his teaching to include an assessment of the intangible.

Challengingly, the accounting treatment of intangibles is often inconsistent and arguably misleading. For example, purchased intangibles are generally treated as an asset, while internally-developed intangibles are generally treated as an expense. Moreover, US GAAP accounting standards treat R&D spending as an expense, while IFRS accounting standards allow the 'D' in R&D to be capitalised as an asset. More generally, there is little prospect of any definitive outcome to these thorny debates among accountants.

For stock investors, it is increasingly clear that grappling with the growth of the intangible is neither easy nor avoidable. Although reasonable people may differ on the detail of the best approach, credible analysis increasingly demands its sensible inclusion.

The Threat to Dollar Dominance

In his insightful 2010 book, *Exorbitant Privilege: The Rise and Fall of the Dollar and The Future of the International Monetary System,* economic historian Barry Eichengreen concludes that the likelihood of continuing US dollar dominance remains high. However, his conclusion comes with one significant, and possibly prescient, *caveat:*

> *Serious economic and financial mismanagement by the United States is the one thing that could precipitate flight from the dollar. And serious mismanagement is not something that can be ruled out. We may yet suffer a dollar crash, but only if we bring it upon ourselves.*

Grappling with the likelihood of such US self-harm, the post-war path of the UK and its troubled currency is instructive.

In 1945, the UK possessed an extensive Empire, formidable armed forces, and a globally significant currency. It was also a nuclear power, a permanent member of the UN Security Council and a major presence across Asia, Africa, and the Middle East. Notwithstanding its relative decline, a future of disproportionate power and prosperity continued to beckon.

But the reckless risk of the Suez Crisis in 1956 – where the threat to Sterling from the Oval Office proved decisive – effectively ended the autonomy of the UK. Never again would it be free to act without the *imprimatur* of the White House. The myopic overestimation of its continuing power had proven calamitous.

By 1976, the UK economy was widely and accurately known as the 'the sick man of Europe'. Mired in industrial strife and with Sterling crashing again, the Callaghan government had little choice but to seek a humiliating IMF bailout in the form of a huge dollar loan. The telling image of Chancellor of the Exchequer Denis Healey at Heathrow Airport, forced to abandon a trip to Hong Kong and return to the Treasury to apply for the loan, captured vividly the loss of power and prestige.

For three quarters of a century, the dominance of the dollar and its unrivalled role as the global reserve currency has been secure. Even the break with gold, and the effective collapse of Bretton Woods in 1971, served only to strengthen rather than to weaken its dominant position.

The more sanitised version of the Obama Doctrine is 'Don't do stupid stuff'. Generally seen as a pithy insight guiding his approach to foreign policy, it arguably summarises the broad approach of post-war US policy in many areas. For decades, as the architect and chief beneficiary of the post-1945 global order, the US adroitly defended and extended the reach and the power of the rules-based multilateral system.

The end of US dominance was never likely to be smooth. But in stark contrast to his post-war predecessors, the most recent occupant of the White House had a radically different view of the power and interests of the US. Under his malign rule, the benign rationality of US engagement with the rest of the world inverted alarmingly.

Despite his departure, the possibility remains that his approach may undermine the dominance of the dollar at the heart of the global monetary system. The salutary experience of the UK highlights the cost of myopic and reckless decisions.

More generally, a new era may be dawning where policymakers and investors across the globe are losing a long-standing constant, while the US faces the loss of a valuable privilege in the ongoing distraction of domestic division.

Like Sterling before it, there is nothing inevitable or immortal about the dominance of the dollar. Expect the calls for a new global monetary order – a new Bretton Woods – to grow louder. While the new President may stem the tide, the days of dollar dominance have seldom seemed as numbered.

The Challenge of Low Bond Yields

In the wake of the Lehman collapse in September 2008, the global economy and banking system faced meltdown. Many feared a re-run of the Great Depression. This view failed to reckon with the powerful tools available to policymakers. More recently, the policy responses to the CoVID-19 pandemic have seen these tools deployed with renewed and expanded aggression.

For example, negative official interest rates are the new normal in Europe and bond investors at every maturity out to 30 years are paying for the privilege of loaning money to many Eurozone governments. More generally, negative real long-term interest rates are now embedded globally.

For long-term investors, this is creating a difficult double challenge: the rising cost of meeting liabilities combined with the falling return on fixed income assets.

At the same time, global stock-markets have been rising strongly. For example, the S&P 500 Index of US stocks recently recorded a new all-time high and is now almost 70% higher than the pandemic-panic low of last March.

This is an especially acute problem for pension funds and insurance companies that traditionally have a very high exposure to fixed income assets for 'risk', regulatory and 'liability matching' purposes.

According to data from Willis Towers Watson, global pension fund assets totalled over $50tn at the end of 2020. The ongoing exposure to negligibly returning cash and fixed income assets is a growing challenge for these funds. Meanwhile, 'general account' (GA) insurance assets are estimated at around $30tn. Once again, the exposure to negligibly returning cash and fixed income assets is a clear and growing challenge. The allocation to such shrinking returns in Europe is especially striking.

The price to earnings ratio is a relationship normally cited for equities. But as a tool for comparing the earnings of any asset with the price of that asset, it can be usefully employed elsewhere. It is after all just the earnings yield inverted.

So, for example, a yield of 1% is a price to earnings ratio of 100 – in other words, a ratio roughly that of the Japanese and Nasdaq stock-markets at their peaks in 1989 and 2000, respectively. Described this way, the large and continuing exposure of long-term pension and insurance investors to fixed income is troubling. The argument that it reduces 'risk' seems especially misplaced.

In a 2006 memo simply called *Risk*, Howard Marks of Oaktree Capital sought to broaden the debate about investment risk from the actuarial and the conventional. In an updated memo in 2018, *Risk Revisited*, he returned to the fray with the crucial insight that:

> *Investors face two major risks: the risk of losing money and the risk of missing opportunities. Either can be eliminated but not both. And leaning too far to avoid one can set you up to be victimized by the other.*

For pension scheme members, trustees, actuaries, and regulators, it's time to stop sleepwalking mechanically into such an outcome. The author and economist, John Kay, has summarised the issue with a typically apt analogy:

> *Do not confuse security with certainty. The man who knows he will be hanged tomorrow has certainty, but not security. His fate is not much more comfortable than that of the saver who today plans to use bonds as a vehicle for retirement saving — the certainty such a*

saver will achieve is the certainty of a low standard of living in old age.

Gyrating Markets & Mental Models

Since the advent of the modern market economy in the early 18th century, the pattern of vaulting boom followed by depressing bust has been a constant. While the details differ, there is little fundamental difference, for example, between the South Sea bubble that so entranced the London of Isaac Newton, and the property bubble that so captured the Ireland of Bertie Ahern.

More recently, investing was a rollercoaster in 2020. Arguably more than ever, the wrenching reality of radical uncertainty was impossible to avoid. Even if we wished it otherwise, the pervasive reach of modern media ensures that market gyrations and frenzied commentary are all but impossible to ignore. Today, the gripping dramas of Bitcoin, Tesla, GameStop, chat-boards, and day-traders seem everywhere.

Charlie Munger is the long-time business partner of Warren Buffett at Berkshire Hathaway and is also a spectacularly successful investor in his own right. Like his more illustrious partner, Munger regularly shares his insights on investing and the wider world. Arguably his most famous insight is 'the latticework of mental models' – a nugget of advice he first shared at the University of Southern California Business School in 1994.

For investors grappling for context and understanding in turbulent times, this insight is particularly helpful:

You've got to have models in your head. And you've got to array your experience – both vicarious and direct – on this latticework of models. You may have noticed students who just try to remember and pound back what is remembered. Well, they fail in school and in life. You've got to hang experience on a latticework of mental models in your head.

Interestingly, this quote inspired portfolio manager Robert G. Hagstrom to write his bestselling book *Investing: The Last Liberal Art* in 2002. Inspired by Munger, Hagstrom explores a range of subjects in the hunt for models relevant to investing, and in a series of timeless insights, he succeeds brilliantly.

More specifically, the author and economist John Kay describes a mental model that may prove especially helpful today.

To shave journey time on the motorway, many drivers employ a 'tailgating' strategy of driving very close to the car in front. Consequently, on almost all trips, they succeed in arriving at their destination sooner, while very occasionally they crash and cause a tragic pile-up. In the aftermath of such a pile-up, there is always a proximate cause offered as an explanation – mechanical failure, driver error, tyre issues or whatever – while the real cause is the 'tailgating' strategy that inevitably results in a pattern of many small gains (time saved) followed by a dramatic loss (crash and pile up).

Kays' 'tailgating' model speaks directly to the current environment. Instead of fruitlessly focussing on the equivalent of mechanical failure, driver error, tyre issues or whatever, stock investors should ponder how they've effectively been speeding dangerously close to the vehicle in front. The real cause of the current drama is less the widely analysed actions of chat-boards and day-traders, and more the extraordinary policy environment that helped propel stock prices ever higher. For investors, by enjoying the gains of such an environment for a prolonged period, perilous exposure to a potential pile up is now unavoidable.

Financial market gyrations are inevitable. Unfortunately, this is not a controversial statement. The undoubted benefits of capitalism only seem available with the unavoidable trauma of periodic upheaval.

Staring into the necessarily unknowable future, there is no reason to expect this pattern to change. But this is not to say that investors are powerless. Taking our cue from the wisdom of Munger, we should develop a 'latticework of mental models'. While exposure to gyrating markets may be unavoidable, informed by the insights of Hagstrom, Kay and others, such models can significantly improve our prospect of profit over loss.

In these frenzied times, the final chapter gives special weight to the undervalued option to hasten slowly, and also seeks to pull it all together by highlighting the top take-aways of this guide.

10

THE UNDER-VALUED OPTION TO HASTEN SLOWLY

In recent weeks, the peripheral world of financial options has charged centre stage. In the dramatic duel between chat-room traders and stock-shorting hedge funds, the role of options has been central and widely discussed.

While the David *vs*. Goliath story has been riveting and the intricacies fascinating, the broader role of optionality for investors deserves greater emphasis. Arguably, the most valuable option of all has been overlooked: doing nothing preserves and protects the option to do something. In effect, all investment decisions are a subjective attempt to price this crucial option.

Nassim Taleb captures this insight characteristically well in his book, *Anti-Fragile: Things That Gain from Disorder*:

> *There is a Latin expression* festina lente, *'make haste slowly'. The Romans were not the only ancients to respect the act of voluntary omission. The Chinese thinker Lao Tzu coined the doctrine of* wu-wei, *'passive achievement'.*

In financial markets that increasingly demand action, the likely benefit of deliberation is easily dismissed. Schooled to quantify and then celebrate action, many scorn inaction as a useless characteristic of the lazy.

By contrast, Taleb celebrates the approach of the Roman general Fabius Maximus. Better known as 'the Procrastinator' for his wise decision to delay fighting the famed Hannibal of Carthage, he waited patiently until time delivered a more favourable shot at victory.

The film *Sliding Doors* was neither a major award winner nor a notable box office success. But the dramatic opening scene starring Gwyneth Paltrow at Holloway Road Tube station has given it an enduring appeal. For investors, the life-changing impact of catching or not catching a given Tube on a given day has a powerful lesson.

Standing on a Tube platform, you must take or not take the Tube before the doors slide shut. As is often the case, the decision to act or not is unavoidable. To their great advantage, investors can effectively freeze time as the Tube stops at the platform with the doors open. They can preserve and protect the option to jump on board or not, until the likely outcome of either decision has become clearer.

For the same reason, the legendary investor and baseball fan Warren Buffett is a great believer in waiting for the 'fat pitch'. He lauds the player with the patience and discipline to wait for the more favourable pitch before deciding to swing. Importantly, the investor with this mindset has the further advantage of never having to worry about being called out. Unlike the baseball player, she can decide to wait, wait, and wait again.

Among much else, John Maynard Keynes was the most famous and influential economist of the 20th century. As the central figure labouring to rebuild the war-ravaged global economy at Versailles and then Bretton Woods, his insights still resonate widely.

Less well-known is his success as an investor. Both for his own account, and as the long-time bursar of his beloved King's College Cambridge, Keynes was exceptionally successful.

From an initial capital sum of £30,000 in 1927, Keynes grew the resources of King's College to £380,000 by the time of his death in 1946. This annual compounding rate of 12% contrasts with the fall of 15% in the overall market over the same period.

Fundamentally, Keynes drew a clear distinction between speculating and investing – in effect, between fast action and patient waiting. Having endured early losses as a speculator, he gave it up as a fruitless pursuit and devoted himself to investing.

Memorably, Keynes's analogy comparing a popular hobby of the time with the challenge of speculating is both timeless, and timely:

> *... a common newspaper game in which the competitors*
> *have to pick out the six prettiest faces from 100*
> *photographs, the prize being awarded to the competitor*

whose choice most nearly corresponds to the average preferences of the competitors as a whole: so that each competitor has to pick, not those faces that he himself finds prettiest, but those that he thinks likeliest to catch the fancy of the other competitors, all of whom are looking at the problem from the same point of view …
We have reached the third degree where we devote our intelligences to anticipating what average opinion expects the average opinion to be. And there are some, I believe, who practise the fourth, fifth, and higher degrees.

If around today, it's safe to assume that Keynes would have little interest in the frenzy of trying to profit from predicting the average opinion of average opinions in violently gyrating stocks.

John Kay is probably best known for his weekly column which ran for many years in the *Financial Times*. More specifically for investors, his updated book, *The Long and the Short of It*, is an enjoyable and accessible summary of his investment approach. As an investor, Kay strongly echoes Keynes. Like the legendary economist, he makes a compelling case against the likelihood of sustainably timing market psychology, dismissing those who claim to do so as lucky, delusional or both.

More than ever in these extraordinary times, investors should beware the pressure to act. Better to ponder the wisdom of Taleb, Buffett, Keynes, and Kay, and to exploit the value of hastening slowly. While the character played by Paltrow at Holloway Road platform or the baseball batsman poised to swing beside the home plate both face an unavoidable time constraint, investors enjoy a rare option to let time be our friend. We should value and use it.

Pulling It All Together: The Top Ten Take-Aways

- There is no return without risk.

- Diversification is crucial – always ponder in portfolio terms.

- Financial markets are efficient, but not wholly so – the market can be beaten.

- Value does not equal price – the market can be beaten.

- Ponder the power of compounding.

- Ponder the thoughts of Taleb.

- Beware the dumb money effect.

- Banks are different – treat them differently.

- Exchange rate risk is unavoidable, but hedging is not necessarily the answer.

- Beware the pressure to act.

Costs

One final issue to ponder is cost. While there is a bewildering array of financial products and advice on offer, we need to have a laser-like focus on cost. Death and taxes may be the great certainties of life, but for investors, unnecessary cost is the great certainty to diminish long-term wealth – be sure to avoid it.

Summary

Financial markets are fascinating but successful investing is not easy. Or to repeat the saltier words of Munger:

It's not supposed to be easy, anyone who finds it easy is stupid!

Hopefully, this short guide will be some help in your search for returns!

BIBLIOGRAPHY

Warren Buffett, *The Super-investors of Graham and Doddsville. Columbia Business School Magazine*, 1984.

Lawrence Cunningham, *The Essays of Warren Buffett: Lessons for Investors and Managers*. John Wiley & Sons, 2009.

Barry Eichengreen, *Exorbitant Privilege: The Rise and Fall of the Dollar and The Future of the International Monetary System*. Oxford University Press, 2011.

John Kenneth Galbraith, *Money: 'Whence It Came, Where It Went*. Princeton University Press, 2007.

Benjamin Graham & David Dodd, *Security Analysis*. McGraw Hill, Sixth Edition, 2008.

Bruce Greenwald, *Value Investing: From Graham to Buffett and Beyond*. John Wiley & Sons, 2001.

Robert G. Hagstrom, *Investing: The Last Liberal Art*, Columbia Business School, 2002.

Jonathan Haskel & Stian Westlake, *Capitalism without Capital: The Rise of the Intangible Economy*. Princeton University Press, 2018.

Daniel Kahneman, *Thinking Fast and Slow*. Farrar, Straus & Giroux, 2011.

John Kay, *Other People's Money: The Real Business of Finance*. Profile Books, 2015.

John Kay, *The Long and the Short of It: A Guide to Finance and Investment for Normally Intelligent People Who Aren't in the Industry*. Profile Books, 2016.

John Maynard Keynes, *The Economic Consequences of the Peace*. Wilder Publications, 2011.

Mervyn King, *Banking: From Bagehot to Basel, and Back Again*. The Second Bagehot Lecture, Buttonwood Gathering, New York, 2010.

Mervyn King, *The End of Alchemy: Money, Banking and the Future of the Global Economy*. Little Brown, 2016.

Seth Klarman, *Margin of Safety: Risk-Averse Value Investing Strategies for the Thoughtful Investor*. Harper Collins, 1991.

Howard Marks, *The Most Important Thing: Uncommon Sense for the Thoughtful Investor*. Columbia University Press, 2011.

Howard Marks, *Risk*. Memos from Howard Marks, 2006.

Howard Marks, *Risk Revisited*. Memo from Howard Marks, 2014.

Hyman Minsky, *The Financial Instability Hypothesis*. Working Paper No. 74, The Jerome Levy Economics Institute of Bard College.

Andrew Oswald, *Herd Behaviour and Keeping up with the Joneses*. CEP 21st Birthday Event: Monday 28 November 2011, Old Theatre, Ground Floor, Old Building, LSE, Houghton Street, London WC2A 2AE.

Mohnish Pabrai, *The Dhando Investor: The Low-Risk Value Method to High Returns*. John Wiley & Sons, 2007.

Nassim Nicholas Taleb, *Fooled by Randomness: The Hidden Role of Chance in Life and in the Markets*. Random House, 2004.

Nassim Nicholas Taleb, *The Black Swan: The Impact of the Highly Improbable*. The Penguin Group, 2007.

Nassim Nicholas Taleb, *Antifragile: Things That Gain from Disorder*. Random House, 2012.

Nassim Nicholas Taleb, *Understanding Is a Poor Substitute for Convexity (Antifragility), Edge,* December 2012.

Richard Thaler, *Misbehaving: The Making of Behavioural Economics*. W.W Norton & Company, 2015.

Richard Thaler & Cass Sunstein, *Nudge: Improving Decision-making about Health, Wealth and Happiness*, Yale University Press, 2012.

Richard Thaler & Shiomo Benartzi, *Myopic Loss Aversion and the Equity Premium Puzzle, Quarterly Journal of Economics*, 1995.

Amos Tversky & Daniel Kahneman, *Judgement Under Uncertainty: Heuristics and Biases. Science,* New Series, Vol. 185, No. 4157. (Sep. 27, 1974), pp. 1124-1131.

ABOUT THE AUTHOR

JOHN LOOBY has been grappling with financial markets for over 30 years. In roles spanning fixed income, absolute return and equities, his fascination with the challenge of investing is undimmed. He is currently a Senior Portfolio Manager on the global equity team at KBI Global Investors. A regular contributor of opinion pieces to the national press – now contributing exclusively to *The Currency* – his previous books are: *Troubled Times: Investing through the Troika Years*, *Sixty Shades of Sunday: Investment Thoughts* and *Money Mayhem: The Bewildering Consequences of Cutting Money Free*. He also lectures part-time at the Dublin Business School. The views expressed in this book are his own.

OAK TREE PRESS

Oak Tree Press develops and delivers information, advice and resources for entrepreneurs and managers. It is Ireland's leading business book publisher, with an unrivalled reputation for quality titles across business, management, HR, law, marketing and enterprise topics.

In addition, Oak Tree Press occupies a unique position in start-up and small business support in Ireland through its standard-setting titles, as well training courses, mentoring and advisory services.

Oak Tree Press is comfortable across a range of communication media – print, web and training, focusing always on the effective communication of business information.

OAK TREE PRESS

E: info@oaktreepress.com
W: www.oaktreepress.com / www.SuccessStore.com.

CPSIA information can be obtained
at www.ICGtesting.com
Printed in the USA
BVHW042317060421
604327BV00010B/535

9 781781 195116